TRADEMARK DESIGNS
OF THE TWENTIES

by

Leslie Cabarga and Marcie Cabarga

DOVER PUBLICATIONS, INC., New York

Copyright © 1991 by Leslie Cabarga and Marcie Cabarga.
All rights reserved under Pan American and International Copyright Conventions.

Published in Canada by General Publishing Company, Ltd., 30 Lesmill Road, Don Mills, Toronto, Ontario.
Published in the United Kingdom by Constable and Company, Ltd., 3 The Lanchesters, 162–164 Fulham Palace Road, London W6 9ER.

Trademark Designs of the Twenties is a new work, first published by Dover Publications, Inc., in 1991.

Manufactured in the United States of America
Dover Publications, Inc., 31 East 2nd Street, Mineola, N.Y. 11501

Library of Congress Cataloging-in-Publication Data

Cabarga, Leslie, 1954–
    Trademark designs of the twenties / by Leslie Cabarga and Marcie Cabarga.
        p.   cm.
    ISBN 0-486-26858-6 (pbk.)
    1. Trademarks—United States—Themes, motives.   2. Design—United States—History—20th century—Themes, motives.   I. Cabarga, Marcie.   II. Title.
    NC998.5.A1C33   1991
    741.6—dc20   91-25477
                                                                                 CIP

PUBLISHER'S NOTE

AN EFFECTIVE TRADEMARK is an invaluable aid to a manufacturer, for it firmly fixes a product in the public's mind, establishing an immense advantage in advertising and sales. Although trademarks date back to ancient times, it was within the past century that the approach we recognize today was fully developed.

The trademarks reproduced on these pages were selected from issues of *The Official Gazette of the United States Patent Office* published (with a few exceptions) during the 1920s. Their publication in the periodical was part of the registration process; it gave a trademark holder the opportunity to contest a new trademark if it "interfered" with his own.

Comprised primarily of combinations of pictorial images with type or calligraphy, the trademarks offer many examples of how designers approached the problem of creating a unique, distinguishing image for a product. The captions, based on information contained in the *Gazette*, list the name of the company applying for registration, the product for which the trademark was intended and the year of the issue in which it appeared.

CONTENTS

1. Domestic Mills Co. (silk), 1921. 2. W. Millender & Sons (leather), 1929. 3. Gordon N. Ferguson, Inc. (hats), 1928. 4. Francis E. Bailey (dresses), 1928. 5. Seals Co. (hosiery), 1929. 6. Sager Glove Co. (leather gloves), 1928. 7. Smith Bros. Importers, Inc. (cravats), 1928. 8. Max Berry (men's suits), 1928. 9. Boss Mfg. Co. (gloves and mittens), 1928.

1. Lewel Mfg. Co. (brassieres), 1928. 2. Eagle Knitting Mills (leather caps), 1928. 3. Schiff Co. (leather shoes), 1929. 4. Ipswich Mills (underwear), 1927. 5. Neely, Harwell & Co. (underwear), 1927. 6. Royal Mfg. Co. (underwear), 1927. 7. Lamborn & Co. (belts), 1920. 8. It Shoe Co. (hose protectors), 1929.

1. Belmont Co. (leather shoes), 1929. **2.** Weber & Lefton, Inc. (ribbons), 1921. **3.** Chas. Chipmanson's Co. (women's hosiery), 1929. **4.** Cheltenham Knitting Co. (underwear), 1928. **5.** Pansy Waist Co. (dresses), 1921. **6.** Huntington Shoe Co. (leather boots), 1921. **7.** Strauss, Adler Co. (brassieres), 1929. **8.** Eugene Byrnes (hosiery), 1921. **9.** Craddock Terry Co. (leather shoes), 1921. **10.** Hartmann-Schneider (overalls), 1929.

1

2

3

4

5

6

7

8

1. E-Z Waist Co. (underwear), 1921. **2.** Cockcroft Silk Co. (silks), 1923. **3.** John A. Pures (human harnesses), 1929. **4.** F. C. Huyck Co. (knitted fabrics), 1921. **5.** Brewer & Co. (athletic supporters), 1929. **6.** Storyk Bros. (dresses), 1929. **7.** Lee J. Barbee Co. (trousers), 1928. **8.** Holman & Franz, Inc. (crepe silk), 1927.

1. Haber's Inc. (men's suits), 1928. 2. W. & A. Turner, Ltd. (sole leathers), 1928. 3. Johnson and Goldstein (men's clothing), 1927. 4. Hickok Manufacturing Co. (belts), 1923. 5. Watts, Ritter & Co. (hosiery), 1920. 6. Harry Felier Co. (men's ties), 1928. 7. Paristyle Button Co. (buttons), 1928. 8. Wright's Clothes, Inc. (overcoats and suits), 1929.

1. The Golden Rule (women's shoes), 1929. 2. Surpass Hosiery Co. (hosiery), 1921. 3. B. Kuppenheimer (coats and vests), 1929. 4. Blackstaff Flax Co. (thread), 1920. 5. James B. Arnold (leather shoes), 1921. 6. American Silk Spinning Co. (spun silk yarn), 1929. 7. Marshall Field & Co. (handkerchiefs), 1929. 8. General Embroidery and Military Supply Co. (emblems), 1928. 9. L. N. Gross Co. (dresses), 1929.

1. L. Heit Co. (clothing), 1929. 2. Midwestern Cap Co. (caps), 1928. 3. Marshall Field & Co. (handkerchiefs), 1929. 4. United Turkey Red Co., Ltd. (cotton piece goods), 1920. 5. Ornstein & Schoenberg (ladies' hats), 1929. 6. Chas. F. Berg Hosiery Co. (hosiery), 1928. 7. Billy Taub (men's suits), 1928. 8. National Wholesale Millinery Co. (ladies' hats), 1928.

1. Ely & Walker Dry Goods Co. (workshirts), 1929. 2. Bencoe Exporting Co. (sheetings), 1920.
3. Associated Buyers, Inc. (dresses), 1928. 4. Etchison Hat Co. (hats), 1928. 5. Otto H. Hinck
(bleached fabrics), 1925. 6. Taylor, Clapp & Beall (cotton sheeting), 1921. 7. Church & Co.
(shoes), 1929. 8. American Thread Co. (cotton thread), 1921.

1. Dip Co. (run-preventing chemical), 1928. 2. E. M. Townsend & Co. (hosiery), 1929. 3. Peggy Jane Mfg. Co. (dresses), 1928. 4. Peacock Shoe Stores Inc. (handbags), 1928. 5. King Chemical Co. (dyes for textiles), 1929. 6. Schiff Co. (leather shoes), 1929. 7. Morris W. Haft Co. (wool and piece goods), 1929. 8. Columbia Mfg. Co. (leather goods), 1928.

1. Wiener & Katz (coats), 1928. 2. George A. Barker (quilts), 1928. 3. Medrick Hosiery Co. (hosiery), 1929. 4. Friedman & Friedman (sleeping garments), 1928. 5. Universal Overalls Co. (men's overalls), 1928. 6. Samuel Brilliant & Co. (leather shoes), 1928. 7. Fashion Shoes Co. (ladies' shoes), 1928. 8. Hollywood Color Co. (shoe dressing), 1928.

1. D. B. Fisk & Co. (women's hats), 1928. 2. Isidor Feldstein (footwear), 1928. 3. Crescent Knitting Co. (hosiery), 1928. 4. Poirette Corsets, Inc. (girdles), 1928. 5. Dieckerhoff Raffloer & Co. (rubber garments), 1927. 6. Angora Specialty Co. (coats and suits), 1920. 7. Providence Braid Co. (shoelaces), 1921. 8. Senack Shoes Co. (shoes), 1928.

1. Crescent Knitting Co. (hosiery), 1928. 2. Leschin Millinery Co. (women's hats), 1926. 3. Baker-Cammack Textile Corp. (workshirts), 1929. 4. Utility Coats, Inc. (ladies' coats), 1929. 5. Tuf-nut Mfg. Co. (negligee shirts), 1928. 6. L. Bamberger & Co. (hosiery), 1929. 7. Sally Frocks, Inc. (frocks and dresses), 1929. 8. Leschin Co. (women's hats), 1926.

1. J. C. Penney Co. (rubber sheets), 1928. 2. Zapon Co. (leather cloth), 1929. 3. Allied Industrial Products (chamois), 1928. 4. Brannigan, Green & Co. (blouses), 1929. 5. May Hosiery Mills, Inc. (hosiery), 1929. 6. Seligman & Katz (hats), 1927. 7. Abraham Rosenblum (embroideries), 1927. 8. F. Ducharne Co. (silk piece skirts), 1929. 9. Durham Hosiery Mills (hosiery), 1929.

1

2

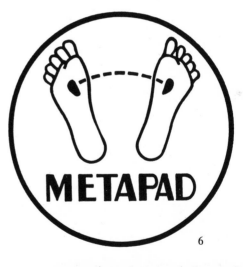

3

5

4

METAPAD

6

Sea Buoy Floater

7

FLEECE BLEND FABRICS

8

1. The Sportswoman, Inc. (sports togs), 1928. 2. Sudan Mercantile Co. (outing dresses), 1929. 3. Acme Shoe Co. (children's shoes), 1928. 4. Soloman Garde (ladies' aprons), 1921. 5. Stauber Co. (aprons), 1921. 6. Haywood Boot Co. (boots and shoes), 1929. 7. Sam Greenberg Co. (life preservers), 1929. 8. McCay Sigler & Taylor Co. (textiles), 1929.

1. Buetzer & Houser Co. (umbrella fabrics), 1929. 2. Lustria Chappell Fills (furs, pelts), 1928.
3. Majestic Curtain Co. (curtains), 1929. 4. Goldstein & Neumann Co. (suits and overcoats),
1919. 5. Hickey-Freeman Co. (men's suits), 1928. 6. Chapline-Myer Shoe Co. (leather shoes),
1929. 7. Wm. H. Hobbs (cotton cloth), 1928. 8. Friedman and Friedman (sleeping garments),
1929. 9. Mission Hosiery Mills (stockings), 1928.

1. Fratelli Markelli (apparel), 1922. 2. May Evelyn Co. (hats for girls), 1921. 3. Henry Fredericks & Co. (camel's-hair coats), 1928. 4. Hair-net Importing Co. (hairnets), 1921. 5. California Tanning Co. (tanned, lace leather), 1929. 6. Derne Co. (dress shirts), 1928. 7. Stern Bros. (leather shoes), 1928. 8. Priscilla Braid Co. (tapes, bindings), 1928. 9. Regent Knitting Corp. (knitted caps), 1921.

Palm Beach Hair Net

Quality Superb

1

Brownie May
WASH FROCKS

2

HIGHLAND

3

THE CARAVAN COAT

4

"SILK of SERVICE"

5

ArchCulture

6

DAY LITE

7

THE YORK

8

1. National Commodities Co. (hairnets), 1918. **2.** Haymon Krupp & Co. (frocks for women), 1929. **3.** The Highland Shoe Co. (boots and shoes), 1929. **4.** Jacob Propose & Sons (camel's-hair coats), 1929. **5.** Frederick Herrschner (silk hosiery), 1927. **6.** Gale Shoe Co. (leather shoes), 1929. **7.** Rubin Bros. (overalls), 1928. **8.** Louis Myers & Son (leather gloves), 1924.

1. Chiquita Coat Co. (coats and suits), 1928. 2. Everett & Barron Co. (footwear polish), 1929.
3. Hahne & Co. (hosiery), 1927. 4. Primfit Textile Co. (hosiery), 1929. 5. Max Nathanson
(apron frocks), 1929. 6. Boris Morris Levine (neckties), 1929. 7. Commodore Shirt Co. (negligee shirts), 1929. 8. Skarloff Bros. (hosiery), 1929. 9. Edward Brownstein (leather shoes), 1926.

Pickwick Shoes

1

Commodore Clothes

2

PLAY PROOF

3

THE
Gold Bond
OLD COLONY SHOE CO.

SHOE

4

PAPERBRELLA

5

NEW YORKER

6

LIONEL SOCKS

7

FEATHER=WEIGHT

8

1. Stewart-Dawes Shoe Co. (shoes), 1928. 2. Bernstein, Schwartz & Co. (men's suits), 1928. 3. Carson, Pirie, Scott & Co. (overcoats), 1928. 4. Old Colony Shoe Co. (leather boots and shoes), 1928. 5. Paperbrella Co. (umbrellas), 1921. 6. Rosen-Brandt, Inc. (ladies' hats), 1928. 7. Mansmann Bros., Inc. (hosiery), 1922. 8. Aerosmith Manufacturing Co. (arch supporters), 1924.

LONGHORN

1

LADDLASSIE

2

BEAU GESTE

3

THREE-AIT DRESSES
888

4

ARCH-RELAXER
FH

5

KENTUCKY
ACE

6

7

WEAR
WORTH

8

1. Dixon-Jenkins Mfg. Co. (overalls), 1928. **2.** Butler Bros. (playsuits for children), 1928. **3.** D. J. Kaufman, Inc. (suits), 1928. **4.** Gimbel Bros. (dresses), 1927. **5.** Frank & Hyman, Inc. (boots, shoes, slippers), 1927. **6.** Southern Kentucky Co. (work clothing), 1927. **7.** A. S. Kreider Co. (leather shoes), 1928. **8.** Carson, Pirie, Scott & Co. (hosiery), 1928.

1. Capitol Silk Corp. (silks), 1928. 2. J. C. Haartz Co. (waterproof fabrics), 1928. 3. United States Fur Auction Brokerage Corp. (furs), 1928. 4. Glico Hosiery Co. (hosiery), 1927. 5. Hero Clothing Mfg. Co. (overcoats), 1928. 6. Morgana Anderson Co. (housefrocks), 1922. 7. Educator Shoe Corp. (leather boots and shoes), 1928. 8. Julius Kayser & Co. (hosiery), 1928. 9. Quix, Inc. (run-preventative product), 1928. 10. Burlington Overall Mfg. Co. (overalls), 1922.

1. The Rival Novelty Co. (children's clothes), 1928. 2. Endicott-Johnson Corp. (leather coats), 1928. 3. B. Altman & Co. (leather shoes), 1927. 4. Welch, Fairchild & Co. (fancy leathers), 1928. 5. Norway Shoe Co. (leather shoes), 1928. 6. Everet & Graff, Inc. (ladies' hats), 1928. 7. Caro Spain Wills (shoes), 1922. 8. Dresvelope Co. (paper garment protectors), 1928. 9. Mutual Knitting Mills (knitted neckties), 1924.

1. New York Hat Stores, Inc. (men's and boys' hats), 1928. 2. Frank L. Pollard Co. (clothes racks), 1922. 3. F. Berg & Co. (felt hats), 1928. 4. Hoyme Co. (bathrobes), 1922. 5. Harry Marx Clothing Co. (men's, boys' coats), 1928. 6. Marcel Franck (hosiery powder), 1928. 7. Darn E-Z Laboratories (hosiery cement), 1922. 8. Jonas Millinery Co. (ladies' hats), 1921.

1. Given Bros. Shoe Co. (shoes), 1928. **2.** Wildfeuer Bros. (leather boots), 1927. **3.** Alpina Leathers (leather goods), 1928. **4.** Peerless Products Corp. (leather refinisher), 1927. **5.** A. B. A. Specialties Co. (garment fasteners), 1927. **6.** The House of Byer (hosiery), 1922. **7.** Crofut & Knapp Co. (hats for men), 1928. **8.** Helen Davis Cap Co. (women's and children's caps), 1928.

1. Montawk Shirt Co. (shirts), 1922. 2. Kaynee Co. (work shirts), 1919. 3. Denburg & Brandenburg (fur garments), 1922. 4. Weeks, Sawyer & Co. (cotton piece goods), 1921. 5. Pippin Co. (poplin shirts), 1925. 6. Ant-I-Wet Corp. (boys' clothes), 1922. 7. Jacob L. Alberts Co. (corsets), 1922. 8. Rex Cap Co. (caps), 1922. 9. Jordan, Marsh Co. (boots and shoes), 1922.

1. Phillipsborn's, Inc. (fabric), 1921. **2.** Packard Hosiery Co. (hosiery), 1922. **3.** John Boyle & Co. (cotton duck), 1922. **4.** Federal Arch-Lift Mfg. Co. (arch supporters), 1922. **5.** S. G. Robinson & Co. (ladies' dresses), 1922. **6.** Jack-O-Way Co. (caps), 1922. 7. I. Isaac & Co. (neckwear), 1924. **8.** Kabuck-Rochester, Inc. (custom-made shirts), 1928.

1

2

SOLITAIRE

3

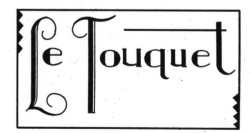

The Garter with the friendly grip

5

The Kind of Clothes
KAHN
MADE TO MEASURE
CLOTHES
Gentlemen Wear

4

IRONMAN

9

Inter-Size

7

Le Touquet

8

Cordcraft
BACKED BY A BOND

6

1. Eltex Fabrics (piece goods), 1928. 2. Morgan Williams Co. (shoes), 1928. 3. Barnet Leather Co. (leather goods), 1928. 4. Kahn Tailoring (men's clothes), 1920. 5. Kleinert Rubber Co. (garters), 1929. 6. Lieberman Co. (trousers), 1921. 7. Inter-Size Dress Co. (gowns), 1928. 8. Rosenfeld Co. (scarfs, dresses), 1928. 9. Wagstaff-Conroy Co. (rubber soles), 1926.

1

3

2

4

Betty Jane FROCKS

6

Thelma

7

Petite Plump

8

1. Chandgie Corp. (silk ties, hosiery), 1927. 2. Schulte-United, Inc. (leather shoes), 1929. 3. Table Art Mat Co. (oilcloth), 1928. 4. Marcy Lee Manufacturing Co. (wash frocks), 1923. 5. R. S. Stern Co. (ladies' hats), 1928. 6. Coast Garment Co. (frocks), 1929. 7. Sussman-Goldstein Co. (hats), 1925. 8. Salomon's Stouts, Inc. (ladies' coats), 1928.

1. Notaseme Hosiery Co. (dolls), 1921. 2. Max Jacobson (talking board game), 1923. 3. Miller Rubber Co. (rubber balls), 1928. 4. Milton Bradley Co. (checkerboards), 1929. 5. The Children's Press (dolls), 1928. 6. National Toys and Tinsel Co. (toy stoves), 1920. 7. Edward Cusack (puzzles), 1928. 8. George Borgfeldt Co. (dolls), 1928.

1

2

MAR·KIT

3

4

B lackbird

5

Dolls—Games
Toys—Puzzles

6

7

8

1. Modern Magic Co. (magic tricks), 1927. 2. Ethel Cochran (dolls), 1929. 3. Kohler Co. (board games), 1929. 4. John Bukolt (pedaling cart), 1919. 5. Penn Products Corp. (clay), 1928. 6. Twinkies Specialty Co. (dolls), 1929. 7. Dean & Williams Co. (toy dump trucks), 1920. 8. Donahue Mfg. Corp. (toys), 1920.

1. R. H. Macy & Co. (chinaware), 1928. 2. Cannon Mfg. Co. (fabric towels), 1921. 3. Cowles Detergent Co. (soap detergent), 1928. 4. Jack E. Brown (washing powder), 1921. 5. Frankart, Inc. (aquariums), 1928. 6. Société Arbox (measuring cups), 1928. 7. Chemical Utilities Co. (wood cleansers), 1920. 8. Rockford Steel Furniture Co. (refrigerators), 1928.

1. Roesch Enamel Range Co. (coal ranges), 1928. 2. Raub Supply Co. (porcelain bathtubs), 1928. 3. Southern Spring Bed Co. (beds), 1929. 4. Oakite Products, Inc. (cleansing detergent), 1929. 5. C. M. Kimball Co. (silver polish), 1921. 6. Deutsche Linoleum Werke (linoleum), 1928. 7. Whiting-Mead Commercial Co. (porcelain enamel bathtubs), 1928. 8. Citizen's Wholesale Supply Co. (cleanser), 1921.

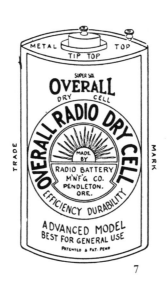

1. London Luggage Corp. (luggage), 1928. 2. H. Gustafson & Co. (washable wallpaper), 1929. 3. Richmond Broom Co. (brooms), 1921. 4. Electric Vacuum Co. (electric vacuum cleaners), 1928. 5. Industrial Home for the Blind (cotton rugs), 1928. 6. Bigler Mfg. Co. (pressed panels), 1928. 7. Radial Battery Mfg. Co. (dry-cell batteries), 1929. 8. Suomen Osuuskauppojen Keskuskunta (safety matches), 1928.

1. Klink Products Corp. (cleaning fluid), 1928. 2. O'Brien & O'Brien (dutch ovens), 1929. 3. J. E. Barbour Co. (twines), 1920. 4. Johnston Household Utilities (can openers), 1929. 5. Standard Oil Co. (paraffin wax), 1929. 6. Cleveland Universal Parts Co. (heaters), 1926. 7. Kroll Bros. Co. (baby carriages), 1929. 8. Morton Mfg. Co. (medicine cabinets), 1928.

1. Rudolph Orthwine (medicine cabinets), 1928. **2.** Central Plumbing Supply Co. (gas ranges), 1929. **3.** Pacific Electrical Products Co. (electric water heater), 1925. **4.** G. S. Blodgett Co., Inc. (bake ovens), 1921. **5.** Electric Bell Range Co. (electric ranges), 1929. **6.** Russel T. Hobbs (cleaning supplies), 1929. **7.** Altofer Bros. Co. (washing machines), 1929. **8.** Kellman Laundry Machinery Co. (clothes-drying machinery), 1925.

1. Vorclone Corp. (dry-cleaning washers), 1929. 2. A. P. W. Paper Co. (paper towels), 1921.
3. Morandi-Proctor Co. (steam tables), 1921. 4. Sentry Co. (heat-treating boxes), 1928. 5. Scott
& Fetzer Co. (electric vacuum cleaners), 1928. 6. Henry Schomer Co. (bed springs), 1921.
7. Palmer Bros. (comforters), 1925. 8. Hanson & Van Winkle Co. (metal polish), 1921.

1

2

CUP

3

4

Dr. Fischer

5

6

8

7

1. Slater's Globe Carpet & Linoleum Co. (linoleum), 1928. 2. Weil-McLain Co. (hot-water radiators), 1928. 3. Geo. Wm. Beldam Co. (rubber sponges), 1920. 4. Revere Electric Co. (electrical supplies), 1928. 5. Michaels Bros. (refrigerators), 1927. 6. Chas. H. Smith (clothes hampers), 1920. 7. David Robinson (ammonia), 1921. 8. Everard L. Wilson (washing compounds), 1921.

1. Noma Electric Corp. (Christmas-tree lights), 1928. 2. Porcelain Products, Inc. (porcelain insulating products), 1927. 3. Universal Lamp Co. (acetylene lamps), 1921. 4. Waco Tool Works, Inc. (electric mixing bowls), 1929. 5. Leslie Co. (metal valves), 1928. 6. United Soap Products Co. (cleanser), 1921. 7. Hibbard Cabinets, Inc. (bottle-cooler cabinets), 1928. 8. Crescent Insulated Wire & Cable Co. (lamps), 1928. 9. Thayer-Telkee Corp. (wall hooks), 1928.

1. Hartman Furniture and Carpet Co. (davenports), 1928. 2. Midwest Refining Co. (furniture polish), 1929. 3. Pepperell Mfg. Co. (bedsheets), 1928. 4. Skandia Furniture Co. (desks), 1928. 5. Wm. F. Roberts (bedsprings), 1926. 6. American Hair and Felt Co. (carpet cushions), 1929. 7. Cleveland Metal Bed Co. (bedsprings), 1928.

Velvet

STAR LOCK

KELDON

1. Artbilt Furniture Co. (Living-room furniture), 1929. 2. Handy Andy Mfg. Co. (nail-file holders), 1928. 3. W. H. Salisbury & Co. (rubber floor tiles), 1922. 4. Star Lock Co. (locks), 1928. 5. Klearflax Linen Looms, Inc. (woolen rugs), 1929. 6. General Electric Co. (glass columns), 1921. 7. Leath & Co. (bedroom furniture), 1928. 8. Annette Moudry (pillows), 1928.

1

2

"LiNO"

3

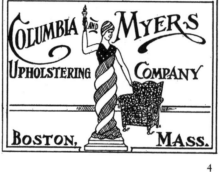

4

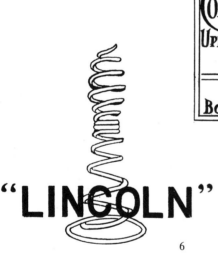

"LINCOLN"

6

BALTIMORE

7

8

1. W. P. Fuller & Co. (mirrors), 1928. 2. Corning Glass Works (lamp globes), 1929. 3. Gunn Furniture Co. (desks), 1921. 4. Columbia and Myers Upholstering Co. (upholstered chairs), 1929. 5. Faultless Caster Co. (furniture casters), 1921. 6. Royal Blue Bed Spring Co. (spring beds), 1929. 7. M. L. Himmel & Sons (tables), 1920. 8. Summerfield Co. (sofas), 1920.

1. Cleveland Metal Bed Co. (bed springs), 1928. **2.** Automatik Chest Co. (metal chests), 1925. **3.** Little Rock Furniture Mfg. Co. (china closets), 1929. **4.** Ellison Furniture & Carpet Co. (mattresses), 1929. **5.** Seville Studios, Inc. (metal benches), 1928. **6.** Congoleum-Nairn, Inc. (inlaid linoleum), 1928. **7.** M. L. Himmel & Sons (garment cabinets), 1920. **8.** Moroccan Importing Corp. (leather cushions), 1929. **9.** I. S. Spencer's Sons (electric lamps), 1929.

SILVER WINGS

1

Smoke CHASERS

2

EXTRA

3

ELLa

5

6

PILGRIM

IMPREGNATED   MADE IN AUSTRIA

SAFETY-MATCHES

4

7

SPORT

8

1. Standard Cigar Co. (cigars), 1928. 2. Bio-Labro Products, Inc. (neutralizer of nicotine odor), 1928. 3. Amtorg Trading Corp. (matches), 1927. 4. Elof Hansson Matches Co. (matches), 1929. 5. Amtorg Trading Corp. (matches), 1926. 6. Hanns A. Widemann (cigarette holders), 1926. 7. Federal Cigar Co. (cigars), 1928. 8. Amtorg Trading Corp. (matches), 1920.

1. Thomas E. Ofiesh (cigarettes), 1928. 2. Willie Brunner Richardson (cigars), 1928. 3. Chase Brass and Copper Co. (filters), 1928. 4. Wales Novelties Corp. (cigarette lighters), 1928. 5. S. S. Pierce Co. (smoking tobaccos), 1929. 6. A. Santaella & Co. (cigars), 1928.

1. Amtorg Trading Corp. (matches), 1928. 2. Segal Lock & Hardware Co., Inc. (pocket and desk lighters), 1928. 3. Universal Tobacco Machine, Co. (tobacco-working machinery), 1921. 4. John C. Herman & Company (cigars), 1920. 5. Amtorg Trading Corp. (matches), 1928. 6. American Tobacco Co. (smoking and chewing tobacco), 1919. 7. Edmund Fridolin Pabst (book matches), 1928.

1

2

3

7

6

8

5

1. National Silver Co. (pyrophoric lighters), 1929. 2. Weidlich Bros. Mfg. Co. (cigarette boxes), 1925. 3. Eduardo Suárez Murias y Compañía (cigars), 1928. 4 & 5. Vulcan Match Co., Inc. (matches), 1929. 6. Silent Automatic Corp. (liquid-fuel burners), 1928. 7. Rapid Manufacturing Co. (lighter fluid), 1928. 8. Lewis Osterweis & Sons (cigars), 1928.

Webster's CHOCOLATE GEMS

1

Amos 'n' Andy

2

CÉSAR

3

4

6

Beech~Nut BESSIE BAR 5¢

5

7

1. Barager-Webster Co. (candy), 1928. 2. Williamson Candy Co. (candy), 1929.
3. Chocolaterie-Confiserie César Société (candy), 1928. 4. Mexican Pecan Candy Co. (candy),
1927. 5. Beech-Nut Packing Co. (candy), 1929. 6. Pugsley Candy Co. (candy), 1929.
7. Curtiss Candy Co. (candy bars), 1928.

YUM-YUM

1

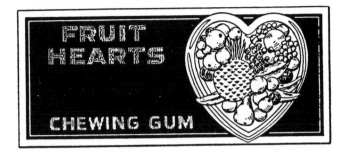

3

Recipe

5

4

6

7

9

8

1. Earl E. LaGrange (chewing gum), 1929. 2. Riesener Chocolate Co. (chocolate candy), 1920.
3. Frank H. Fleer Corp. (chewing gum), 1929. 4. Valentino Candy Co. (candy), 1928.
5. CrackerJack Co. (candy), 1928. 6. Williamson Candy Co. (candy), 1929. 7. Tiffany & Co.
(candy), 1928. 8. E. L. Mathews Co. (candy), 1929. 9. Perkins Co. (candy), 1921.

1. W. Watson Co. (chocolate-covered potato chips), 1928. 2. Walter Birk Co. (candy), 1928. 3. W. E. Jacobs Candy Co. (candy), 1928. 4. C. T. Fund Co. (candy), 1927. 5. Sunshine Purity Ice Cream Co. (ice cream), 1929. 6. Herbert A. Meyers Candy Co. (chewing gum), 1928. 7. California Consumers Co. (candy), 1929. 8. Williamson Candy Co. (candy), 1928.

WHIZ BANG

1

Chocolate Honeys

Chocolate Honeys

Chocolate Honeys

2

Oh!-Oh!

3

The **FREEZER** **FUDGE**

4

5

LONG CHEW GUM

WORLD'S LONGEST CHEW!

6

Puffles

7

OCEAN ROLL

8

1. Fleer Corp. (chewing gum), 1927. 2. Fair Play Caramels (candy), 1927. 3. Williamson Candy Co. (candy), 1928. 4. The Freezer Co. (fudge), 1927. 5. Continental Candy Corp. (candy), 1920. 6. Clarke Bros. Chewing Gum Co. (chewing gum), 1928. 7. Puffles Inc. (candy confections), 1928. 8. G. L. Walker Co. (candy), 1927.

DRAKE'S

1

2

TRADE MARK

3

Hidden Secret Confections

TURKEY TROTS

4

VANILLA CHOCOLATE

5

Princess Pat

6

8

7

1. L. M. Carr (candy), 1922. **2.** Homer J. Williamson (candy), 1922. **3.** Wisconsin Candy Co. (chocolates), 1921. **4.** Peerless Confection Co. (candy), 1928. **5.** Runkel Bros. Inc. (vanilla and chocolate), 1922. **6.** Queen Anne Candy Co. (coconut bar candy), 1922. **7.** Tangermunder Co. (candied fruit), 1926. **8.** Chas. H. Younger (almond brittle), 1928.

Du Barry
1

Rough Bar
2

HOB NOBS CONFECTIONS
3

4

TOROS
5

Close's
7

PORK CHOP
6

HAZEL KNUT
8

1. S. H. Kress & Co. (assorted chocolates), 1928. 2. Parisian Chocolate Co. (candy), 1922. 3. Robt. G. Lindsay (chewing gum), 1928. 4. Crystal Candy Co. (candy), 1922. 5. Mason Confectionery Co. (candy), 1922. 6. Puritan Candy Co. (candy), 1928. 7. George Close Co. (candy), 1928. 8. Michael Economos Candy Co. (candy bars), 1922.

1. Shreveport Syrup Co. (table syrup), 1928. 2. Hahn & Livingston Co. (fruit), 1928. 3. Rein Co. (ice), 1928. 4. Maggi Co. (soups), 1921. 5. H. C. Brill Co. (cake), 1929. 6. Giles-Cummings Co. (butter), 1928. 7. C. F. Schobert Co. (peanut butter), 1929. 8. Kentucky Vegetable Growers Assoc. (fresh vegetables), 1928.

1. Mrs. O. A. Knight (nut spread), 1928. 2. A. Goldstein Co. (canned fish), 1925. 3. Neighbor Products Co. (macaroni), 1927. 4. Doughnut Machine Corp. (doughnut mixture), 1928. 5. Premier Machinery Co. (vegetable peelers), 1921. 6. H. C. Brill Co. (cake), 1929. 7. Lummis & Co. (salted peanuts), 1928. 8. H. C. Hallam (malt syrup), 1928.

1. Walter's Packing Co. (salted peanuts), 1928. 2. Ross Milling Co. (wheat flour), 1922.
3. Queensbury Farms (eggs), 1922. 4. Pacific Grape Co. (canned fruits), 1928. 5. Katz Flour
Co. (wheat flour), 1922. 6. Boonville Mills Co. (wheat flour), 1922. 7. California Prune and
Apricot Growers Assoc. (dried fruits), 1922. 8. Poage-Wall Milling Co. (wheat flour), 1922.

1. General Baking Co. (bread), 1921. 2. C. Wilkins Co. (mayonnaise), 1920. 3. Burnett, Kraft & Kauffman Milling Co. (wheat flour), 1921. 4. Red Sun Products Co. (malt extracts), 1922. 5. Dutch Maid Flour Co. (wheat flour), 1928. 6. Mountain States Honey Producers' Assoc. (comb honey), 1928. 7. General Baking Co. (bread), 1921. 8. Vita Food Co. (medicated food), 1920.

1. Garrett Co. (fresh grapes), 1928. 2. Pioneer Creamery Co. (butter and eggs), 1921. 3. Dunlop Milling Co. (wheat flour), 1922. 4. Mizell Murrey Co. (rolled oats), 1921. 5. General Baking Co. (bread), 1921. 6. S. W. Hershey Flour Mills (wheat flour), 1922. 7. Standard Tilton Milling Co. (wheat flour), 1922. 8. Southern Peanut Co. (fried peanuts), 1928.

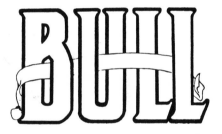

1. Quisenberry Feed Mfg. Co. (poultry feed), 1922. 2. Oakland Noodle Factory (soy sauce), 1928. 3. Boston Molasses Co. (molasses), 1922. 4. Farnsworth Packing Co. (canned sardines), 1922. 5. Wagner Pastry Co. (pies), 1923. 6. Perry O. Clark (fresh grapes), 1922. 7. Southern Ice Co. (manufactured ice), 1928. 8. North Shore Specialty Co. (canned marshmallows), 1921.

SHOSHONE

4

1. Kerr Chickeries, Inc. (live chicks), 1922. 2. Beauty Cone Co. (ice-cream cones), 1928. 3. Federal Mill & Elevator Co. (wheat flour), 1923. 4. Globe Grain & Milling Co. (wheat flour), 1926. 5. W. Lee Gordon Co. (potato chips and popcorn), 1924. 6. C. M. Ryder (butter, eggs), 1925. 7. Lawrenceberg Roller Mills Co. (scratch feed), 1922.

1. Tampa Rice Co. (rice), 1928. 2. Walter S. Dailey Co. (frozen confections), 1922.
3. Washburn-Cosby Co. (wheat flour), 1921. 4. Henry A. Orthmann (mayonnaise dressing),
1923. 5. Aunt Jemima Mills Co. (wheat flour), 1922. 6. Sussman, Wormser & Co. (dairy
products), 1922. 7. Polar Gate Co. (ice cream), 1925. 8. C. Basilea Co. (olive oil), 1923.

1. Milk Producers' Assoc. of Central California (evaporated milk), 1927. 2. Albers Bros. Milling Co. (pastry flour), 1928. 3. R. Hickmott Canning Co. (canned asparagus), 1928. 4. Cremo Pop Corp. (chocolate coatings), 1928. 5. Blair Milling Co. (wheat flour), 1921. 6. R. T. French Co. (herbs), 1928. 7. Sears and Nicholls Corp. (canned tomatoes), 1927. 8. Wm. G. Roe (citrus fruits), 1929.

1. Colorado Milling & Elevator Co. (wheat flour), 1929. 2. C. Cretors Co. (butter substitute), 1928. 3. Gahan Baking Co. (doughnuts), 1919. 4. Spreckles Baking Co. (sugar), 1929. 5. Bert Scott (fresh vegetables), 1927. 6. Friedman & Bruno (fresh vegetables), 1928. 7. Sgobel & Day, Inc. (fresh fruit), 1921. 8. Chester H. Johnson (dehydrated citrus fruits), 1920.

1. Goodrich Bakeries, Inc. (pies), 1928. 2. Sociedad Anónima Frigorífico Anglo (canned corned beef), 1927. 3. Alfred J. Richie (canned fruits), 1927. 4. Beaver Produce Co. (butter and eggs), 1928. 5. Western Grocery Co. (table salt), 1929. 6. Mitchell Silliman Co. (fresh vegetables), 1928. 7. Mulkey Salt Co. (salt), 1926. 8. Lindorff Mfg. Co. (gravy), 1928.

1. Sexton Co. (baked goods), 1928. 2. Lake Charles Rice Milling Co. (rice), 1927. 3. Reynolds and Irving Co. (cheese), 1926. 4. Peter N. Papason (groceries), 1920. 5. Keebler-Weyl Baking Co. (cookies), 1928. 6. John T. McNaney (raw oysters), 1927. 7. Cardwell Brokerage Co. (Irish potatoes), 1928. 8. Sequoia Foothills Fruit Growers (fresh grapes), 1929.

1. OK Peanut Butter Co. (peanut butter), 1928. 2. Southern Dairies, Inc. (ice cream), 1928.
3. S. Gumpert Co. (cakes), 1928. 4. Cresca Co. (French crackers), 1926. 5. Colorado Milling
& Elevator Co. (wheat flour), 1922. 6. United Bi-Products Co. (hog feed), 1928. 7. Aviation
Food Mfg. Co. (mayonnaise), 1928. 8. The Friedman-Kerr Co. (candy), 1922. 9. Harry W.
Studt (mayonnaise), 1928.

1. Hugo Bruni Co. (malt syrup), 1928. **2.** Hawaiian Pineapple Co. (canned fruits), 1928. **3.** Stanley Fruit Co. (fresh lettuce), 1928. **4.** Emmental Cheese Corp. (cheese), 1927. **5.** Goody Nut Shops (salted nuts), 1928. **6.** G. Palmisani & Co. (olive oil), 1928. **7.** J. B. Car Bisquit Co. (biscuits), 1920. **8.** Kelly-Clarke Co. (canned fish), 1928.

FARWELL &RHINES

Quick
**CAKE AND
WAFFLE FLOUR**

1

WAT A JOY

2

LIBERTY BELL

4

GEE
It's Good!

3

Lucrativa

5

ROMAN

6

FIRE ARROW

7

RED WING

8

1. Farwell & Rhines Co. (wheat flour), 1928. 2. John Huber Co. (cakes), 1928. 3. Aubrey's Bakery (bread), 1928. 4. Teagarden Products Co. (maple syrup), 1928. 5. Maniello Bros., Inc. (fresh apples), 1928. 6. Roman Meal Co. (cereal and bread), 1927. 7. Thom-Body Co. (canned fruits), 1920. 8. Redwing Corp. (dairy products), 1920.

Baker MAID

1

RIVER BRAND

2

The Maramor

3

Blue Moon

5

"HIME"

4

6

BLUE BAND MALT SYRUP

7

IDEAL

PURE WINTER WHEAT BRAN

8

1. Horace Baker (vegetable soups), 1929. 2. Southern Rice Co. (rice), 1929. 3. Maramor Co. (candies, cakes, bread), 1928. 4. Pacific Trading Co. (bamboo sprouts), 1928. 5. John S. Beckwith Co. (peaches), 1929. 6. United Rabbitries Marketing Co. (rabbit stew), 1928. 7. Home Extract Co. (malt syrup), 1928. 8. Burnett, Kraft & Kauffman Milling Co. (bran), 1928.

1. Aviston Milling Co. (wheat flour), 1927. 2. Rudy Patrick Seed Co. (rolled oats), 1929.
3. Pacific Trading Co. (rice), 1929. 4. Puritan Ice Cream Co. (ice cream), 1921. 5. Kansas
Milling Co. (wheat flour), 1928. 6. Griggs, Cooper & Co. (peanut butter), 1928.
7. Aktiebolaget Arvid Petterssons Co. (bread), 1928. 8. Edwardsville Creamery Co. (nut short-
ening), 1929. 9. Griggs, Cooper & Co. (syrup), 1928.

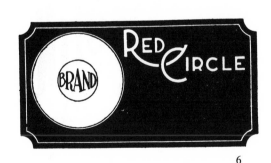

1. Jersey Farm Products Co. (malt syrup), 1929. **2.** Blamberg Bros. Inc. (poultry), 1921. **3.** Raflax Products Co. (health biscuits), 1928. **4.** George H. Willet (milk), 1929. **5.** Pabst Corp. (malt syrup), 1928. **6.** Detroit Beef Co. (butter and eggs), 1920. **7.** Doctors' Essential Foods Co. (bread), 1920.

Discovery

1

Fluffy Down

2

A McCann "Puritan" Turkey

3

RUSSKIY **R**EAL **R**USSIAN R**YE**

4

Morrells Pride

5

Wienie Mint

6

BANJO

7

9

Blue Pigeon

8

1. Kelley-Clarke Co. (canned salmon), 1927. 2. Ansted & Burke Co. (wheat flour), 1928.
3. McCann & Co. (dressed turkeys), 1929. 4. Wm. H. Brooks (bread and crackers), 1928.
5. John Morell & Co. (luncheon meat), 1921. 6. Arnold Bros., Inc. (food heaters), 1928.
7. Hezel Milling Co. (self-rising flour), 1921. 8. John L. Seibel Co. (fresh grapes), 1928. 9. The
Dugout (sandwiches), 1929.

C. and H.

CHICKEN GREENS

1

2

The BLUE BOOK

3

EZ COOKERS

4

SUN-MAID

FROZEN BETTY

5

SUN BLOOM

6

Oldtyme

OPEN KETTLE MOLASSES

7

Snow Fairy

8

BLUE EARTH

9

1. California-Hawaiian Mills (chicken feed), 1928. 2. Sun Maid Raisin Growers (raisins), 1929.
3. The Smith and Chinn Co. (fresh vegetables), 1929. 4. C. Knoke & Co. (split peas), 1928.
5. Southern Cone Co. (chocolate-covered frozen fruits), 1928. 6. Kern County Growers (fresh
fruits), 1929. 7. Sugar Products Co. (molasses), 1920. 8. Walnut Creek Milling Co. (wheat
flour), 1928. 8. Blue Earth Canning Corp. (canned vegetables), 1928.

1. Vim Food Products Co. (chocolate malted milk), 1929. 2. Corkran Hill & Co. (ham), 1928.
3. Mystic Mills (wheat flour), 1928. 4. Pre-cooling Car Service Co. (fresh vegetables), 1927.
5. D. L. Page Co. (salad dressing), 1928. 6. H. H. Packing Co. (fruit), 1928. 7. Mennel Milling
Co. (wheat flour), 1928. 8. D. D. Scully Syrup Co. (table syrup), 1929.

1

2

3

4

5

6

7

8

1. Town Talk Sandwich Shops (sandwiches), 1928. 2. American Tripoli Co. (flour), 1920.
3. Geo. Morrison's Co. (jams and jellies), 1928. 4. Arnold Bros. (pickles and preserves), 1928.
5. Ransom Grain & Coal Co. (rabbit food), 1928. 6. Big Diamond Mills Co. (wheat offals),
1926. 7. Muscle-Malt Products (malt extract), 1928. 8. American Cone & Pretzel Co. (pretzels), 1928.

1. Fratelli Berio (olive oil), 1928. 2. Union Biscuit Co. (sugar wafers), 1922. 3. Dainty Maid Co. (relish), 1922. 4. Holland–O'Neill Milling Co. (wheat flour), 1925. 5. Pacific Coast Biscuit Co. (crackers), 1922. 6. Alexander Gallerina Co. (macaroni), 1922. 7. Salinas Valley Canning Co. (canned fruits), 1928. 8. Pacific Coast Biscuit Co. (crackers), 1921. 9. Dixie Baking Co. (bread), 1928.

1

Sweetangood

2

No Joke

3

Surety BREAD

4

5

GREEN FARMS

6

Mickelberry's
Old Farm Brand

7

1. Strohmeyer & Arpe Co. (canned sardines), 1926. 2. Matthaei Baking Co. (cookies), 1922.
3. Phillip James Langford (citrus fruit), 1921. 4. General Baking Co. (bread), 1921. 5. C.
Perceval (cheeses), 1922. 6. Penick & Ford, Ltd. (maple syrup), 1928. 7. Mickelberry's Food
Products (sausage), 1922.

1. Orange-Crush Co. (maltless beverages), 1928. **2.** Nathan K. Ross (beverages), 1922.
3. Cauchois Coffee Co. (cocoa), 1928. **4.** Jack Beverage Co. (beverages), 1922. **5.** Star Beverage
Co. (beverages), 1919. **6.** O. R. Randall (beverages), 1928. **7.** Western Milk Co. (evaporated
milk), 1928. **8.** The Ver-Vac Co. (fruit syrups), 1922. **9.** Abner-Drury Co. (ginger ale), 1922.

1. American Milk Products Corp. (sweetened milk), 1922. 2. William Neis & Son (ginger ale), 1928. 3. Victor Mfg. Co. (maltless beverages), 1922. 4. Mihran Basmagian (cocoa), 1928. 5. Fred F. Korn (maltless beverages), 1928. 6. Twin Springs Mineral Water Co. (ginger ale), 1928. 7. Coca-Cola Bottling Co. (soft drinks), 1922. 8. Pale Moon Co. (maltless beverages), 1928.

1. Universal Milk Co. (evaporated milk), 1928. 2. Louis Fine (maltless beverages), 1928.
3 S. C. Wells & Co. (herb tea), 1928. 4. J. F. Lazier Mfg. Co. (ginger ale), 1928. 5. American
Cuptor Corp. (soft-drink vending machines), 1928. 6. Cedar Rapids Bottling Works (ginger ale),
1928. 7. Anderson Co. (maltless beverages), 1921. 8. Irving McEwen (ginger ale), 1928.

1. Val Blatz Brewing Co. (malt beverages), 1929. 2. Union Bottling Works (maltless beverages), 1928. 3. Joseph Bump Co. (orange-flavored soft drink), 1918. 4. Goldelle Ginger Ale Co. (ginger ale), 1921. 5. Queen City Bottling Co. (maltless beverages), 1921. 6. Coral Rock Ginger Ale Co. (ginger ale), 1928. 7. Love Bottling Co. (soft drinks), 1928. 8. St. Paul Bottling Co. (ginger ale), 1929.

1. Belmont Products Co. (malt extract), 1929. 2. Benjamin Franklin Booth (maltless beverages), 1921. 3. Iroquois Beverage Co. (cereal beverages), 1921. 4. Kingsway Corp. (fruit juices), 1928. 5. Goody Nectar Co. (maltless beverages), 1928. 6. Los Angeles Brewing Co. (maltless beverages), 1928. 7. Malt-O-Milk Co. (chocolate malted milk), 1921. 8. Bridgeport Bottling Co. (sarsaparilla), 1928.

1

2

3

THE HOP LEAF

4

5

MIRAKEL

6

Old Keg

7

8

1. Shasta Water Co. (maltless beverages), 1928. 2. Tauber Co. (food beverage powder), 1928.
3. Richards & Co. (cocoa syrup), 1924. 4. H. & G. Simonds Co. (malt beverages), 1928.
5. Alfred Smith (soft drinks), 1928. 6. Mirakel Products Co. (coloring/flavoring for beverages),
1926. 7. Excelsior Brewerie Inc. (malt beverages), 1928. 8. Kentucky Nip Corp. (carbonated
beverages), 1928.

1. Hyman Matrick Co. (instant coffee), 1929. 2. Fort Smith Coffee Co. (coffee), 1921. 3. Shear Coffee Co. (coffee), 1928. 4. Pearl Coffee Co. (coffee), 1920. 5. Bindley Grocery Co. (coffee), 1928. 6. Donut Machine Corp. (coffee), 1928. 7. Harry Stahl, Inc. (coffee cake), 1921. 8. R. S. Gehlert & Co. (coffee), 1928.

1. Vinson Coffee Co. (coffee), 1921. 2. Holland Coffee Co. (coffee), 1929. 3. B. B. Bickers (coffee), 1928. 4. Spray Coffee & Spice Co. (roasted coffee), 1927. 5. Great Atlantic & Pacific Tea Co. (coffee and chicory compound), 1928. 6. American Stores Co. (coffee), 1928. 7. Merkle Coffee Co. (coffee), 1929. 8. U.S. Coffee & Tea Co. (tea and coffee), 1927. 9. Arabian Coffee Co. (coffee), 1928.

1. Megargee Bros. (toilet paper), 1928. 2. Eau de Cologne (toilet soaps), 1928. 3. Nell Oliver Co. (soap), 1928. 4. People's Drug Stores (cosmetics), 1928. 5. J. H. Schmidt, Inc. (nail polish), 1928. 6. Laila Fleur, Inc. (hand lotion), 1928. 7. Pinaud, Inc. (toilet water), 1928. 8. Oxol Products Co. (antiseptic), 1928.

1. Duradene Co. (hair-waving solution), 1928. 2. Sheffield Bronze Powder Co. (bronze powder), 1928. 3. Agnes L. Vierra (rubber protector), 1928. 4. Hutchinson Co. (face-cleaning cloth), 1928. 5. Acme Labs, Inc. (skin creams), 1927. 6. People's Drug Stores (toilet water), 1928. 7. Gerre, Inc. (astringents), 1928. 8. Proctor & Gamble Co. (soap), 1928.

TUX

JAMES
SURRATTS

1. George Paganist (hair tonic), 1922. **2.** Joseph Avina (perfume), 1928. **3.** Mackie Pine Oil Specialty Co. (hair shampoo), 1928. **4.** Ilon/Adler (oil shampoos), 1928. **5.** Gallagher-Thomas Chemical Co. (hair tonics), 1928. **6.** Lenna Therress Alexander (hair tonic), 1922. **7.** Leopold Weber (liquid shampoo), 1922. **8.** Ogilvie Sisters (liquid powder), 1922.

Bull Dog

2

3

4

5

LaVion-Etie

6

7

8

9

1. Charles A. Crary (toilet soap), 1928. **2.** Hannover Rubber Co. (combs), 1928. **3.** Andis O. M. Mfg. Co. (hair clippers), 1921. **4.** Wortendyke Mfg. Co. (toilet paper), 1928. **5.** S. P. M. Co. (powder puffs), 1922. **6.** Milton Kahn Co. (face powder), 1928. **7.** Charles L. Klapp (face powder), 1921. **8.** LaSalle Co. (hair tonic), 1922. **9.** Henry J. Pressenger (deodorant), 1928.

1. Yvette Co. (hair lotions), 1928. 2. Turmel Co. (hair dyes), 1928. 3. Laura Hair Novelty Co. (sanitary napkins), 1929. 4. Cleaning Products Co. (hand soap), 1928. 5. Parfumerie Caron (perfume), 1929. 6. Bercy's Laboratories (astringents), 1928. 7. Mohammed I. Kitchlew (perfume), 1927. 8. Veldown Co. (paper neckbands), 1927.

Swanfleece

Kremer's Youth

Frezo

DYM-NO-SMEL

Super Curline

MOTAS ESTRELLA

SILVER MOON

THE KAUFFMAN SANITARY · POCKET SPITKUP · JENNY

1. Veldown Co. (toiletries), 1928. 2. George Kremer Co. (bleach creams), 1928. 3. Corinna, Inc. (shaving cream), 1928. 4. Dym-No-Smel Co. (deodorants), 1928. 5. Paul Gaire Co. (hair-waving machines), 1928. 6. F. Tetter & Sons (powder puffs), 1928. 7. Silver Moon Specialty Co. (nail polish), 1928. 8. Jacob Kauffman Co. (sanitary cups), 1925.

1. Arthur Anderson (tooth powder), 1929. 2. Gladiator Co. (hair tonic), 1928. 3. Superior Products Co. (face powder), 1928. 4. Guillaume Bailet (hair dye), 1922. 5. Hartmann Chemical Co. (cold cream), 1928. 6. Barklay & Co. (soap), 1922. 7. Crysto Soap Co. (mineral soap), 1922. 8. Hatton Mfg. Co. (hair tonic), 1922.

1. Charméne Beauty Products (permanent-waving pads), 1929. 2. George James Southworth (skin cream), 1922. 3. Sea-Dip Co. (bath salts), 1922. 4. Paul Westphal Co. (hair tonic), 1922. 5. Fort Orange Chemical Co. (hand soap), 1922. 6. Kauffman Bros. (hair nets), 1921. 7. R. J. Watkins Co. (soap flakes), 1928. 8. Cudahy Soap Works (toilet soap), 1922. 9. Joseph Amster (razor blades), 1928.

1. C. A. Swanson Drug Co. (beauty lotion), 1929. 2. Onofrio Zacamy Co. (hair tonic), 1929. 3. Metropolitan Hair Goods Co. (hair nets), 1921. 4. Palmolive Co. (soap), 1921. 5. Plough Chemical Co. (cold cream), 1928. 6. George C. Spencer (perfumes), 1921. 7. Whiteford E. McMillan Co. (deodorizers), 1921. 8. Wm. Tyler Green Co. (beauty cream), 1921.

1. Abram Kairy Co. (astringents), 1928. 2. Ethel Thornton Supply Co. (witch hazel), 1929.
3. Pond's Extract Co. (tissues), 1927. 4. Nathan B. Cohen (hair nets), 1921. 5. James S. Livesay
Co. (hair tonic), 1921. 6. Paris Co. (toilet water), 1929. 7. Pond's Extract Co. (cold cream), 1927.
8. Hygienic Products Co. (water softener), 1927. 9. Primrose Laboratories (rouges), 1929.

1. Louis I. Block Co. (skin preparation), 1926. **2.** Winsor Soap Co. (castile soap), 1928.
3. Scott's Preparations, Inc. (facial massage cream), 1920. **4.** Boldoot Co. (buttermilk soap),
1916. **5.** Hardright Co. (lather brushes), 1920. **6.** Robertson Products Co. (liquid soap), 1929.
7. Illinois Razor Strop Co. (razor strops), 1909. **8.** Mitchell Wing Co. (face cream), 1929.

1. Smith, Kline & French Co. (lactose preparation), 1929. 2. Gifford Co. (acne cream), 1926. 3. Irving W. Rice Co. (hair nets), 1921. 4. John C. LaRosa Co. (hair tonic), 1928. 5. Melba Manufacturing Co. (perfumes), 1919. 6. Morton Labs (sunburn lotion), 1929. 7. VanAntwerp's Drug Co. (face powder), 1916. 8. International Consolidated Chemical Co. (face lotions), 1921. 9. Georgia A. Swan Co. (cold cream), 1928.

1. Richard Hudnut, Inc. (soap), 1928. 2. Paramount Specialty Co. (toilet paper), 1927.
3. California Beauty Products (face powder), 1928. 4. Cowles Detergent Co. (detergent), 1928.
5. Morris Seder Co. (hair tonics), 1919. 6. Lucille Buhl Co. (powder puffs), 1928. 7. Ritzie Co.
(beautifying lotion), 1927. 8. Calber Co. (toilet soap), 1926. 9. DuPont Viscaloid Co. (hair-brushes), 1928.

1. Annette Knapp Co. (face pack), 1919. 2. Fred J. Silk (canned soap), 1928. 3. Removo Co. (gray-hair restorer), 1920. 4. Hayfay Laboratories (dentrifice), 1921. 5. Metropolitan Safety Razor Co. (safety razors), 1929. 6. Myrtle Merz Maharon Co. (douche powder), 1928. 7. Clayton & Young (deodorant and foot preparation), 1928. 8. Eugene, Ltd. (permanent-waving machines), 1926. 9. Excelsior Co. (combs), 1929.

1. Dr. J. L. Pyle (headache tablets), 1929. 2. Edwin S. Veatch Co. (rheumatism pills), 1929.
3. Adson Chemical Co. (nasal inhalant), 1928. 4. John DeCock's Co. (blood-purifying herbs),
1928. 5. Elias Lipiner Co. (salves), 1928. 6. Antonia R. Martino (laxatives), 1928. 7. The Rex-
A-Cold Laboratories (cold pills), 1929. 8. Henry C. Jarvis (constipation pills), 1921.

1. Langley & Michaels Co. (citrate of magnesia), 1929. **2.** Dr. Richards Assoc. (medicine), 1929. **3.** Lawrence Lederer (rubber appliances), 1928. **4.** Soderseine Co. (medicine), 1921. **5.** Medicinal Products Co. (corn pomade), 1929. **6.** Harry M. Griffin Co. (headache remedy), 1920. **7.** Poth & Kuener Co. (piles remedy), 1921. **8.** Nutlax Co. (laxative), 1926.

1. Francis L. Holliday Co. (treatment of asthma), 1920. 2. Frank O'Neill Co. (medicinal tonic), 1924. 3. Standard Medical Co. (ointment for headcolds), 1929. 4. Chicago Flexible Shaft Co. (therapeutic lamps), 1929. 5. George Robbins Co. (ointment for hemorrhoids), 1921. 6. Southern Mineral Corp. (germicidal antiseptic), 1928. 7. Ernest F. Mattutat Co. (hemoglobin tablets), 1921. 8. Alderic Desaint·Co. (medicines), 1920.

1. Jayzon's Co. (cod-liver oil), 1928. 2. John A. Morey Co. (nostril salve), 1929. 3. Edwin C. Miller Co. (medicines), 1927. 4. Food Balance Corp. (medicine), 1928. 5. Drug Products Co. (analgesics), 1920. 6. Sloan, Inc. (liniment), 1921. 7. Herbert A. Berring Co. (colic medicine), 1929. 8. ABC Products Co. (liniment), 1929. 9. Wm. H. Luden (menthol cough drops), 1921.

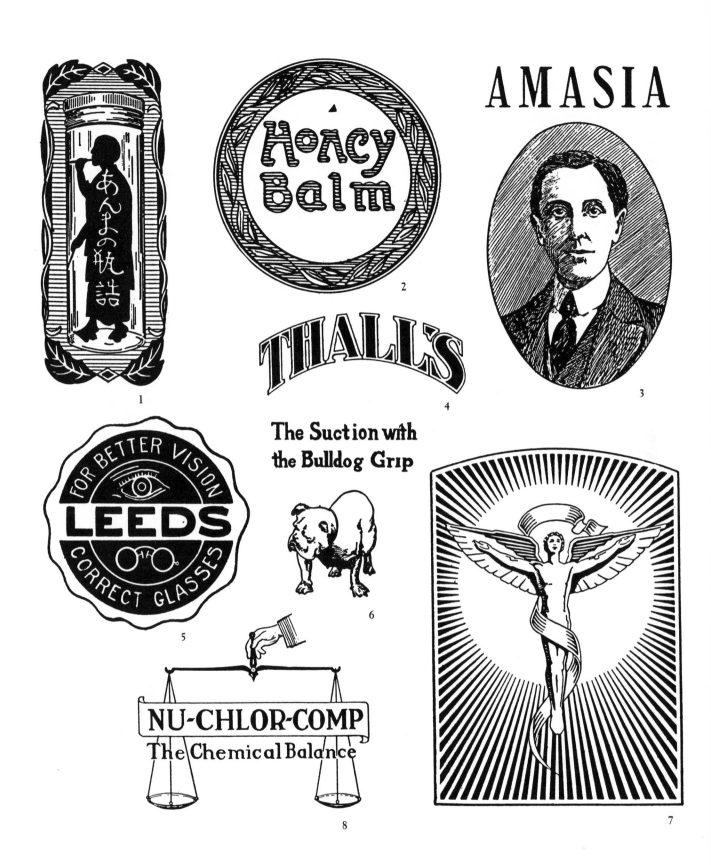

1. Tamisuke Kino Co. (rheumatism medicine), 1928. 2. Costas Gekas (gonorrhea medicine), 1921. 3. Amasia Co. (medicines), 1920. 4. David Thall (iron syrup), 1929. 5. Max Kaplan Co. (lenses), 1928. 6. John Lehner (dental plates), 1919. 7. American Society of Chiropractors (books and pamphlets), 1929. 8. Nu-Chlor Chemical Co. (antiseptic), 1929.

1. Dr. Miles Medical Co. (sedatives), 1929. 2. American Drug Co. (tonic), 1921. 3. Silvan Maurice Edison (healing balm), 1929. 4. Morris S. Michael (salves for colds), 1928. 5. Great Northern Supply Co. (medicine), 1920. 6. Antiseptic Pharmacal Co. (medicine), 1926. 7. Rumford Chemical Works (tonic), 1928. 8. Plentiwood Drug & Co. (medicine for stomach ulcers), 1928.

1. Francis W. Kurtz & Co. (eyeglasses), 1928. 2. Seminole Remedy Co. (rheumatism medicine), 1922. 3. Hollinger Remedy Co. (medicine), 1928. 4. Lee-Mar Co. (liniment), 1928. 5. Brothers Corp. (analgesics), 1928. 6. Teutonia Eye Salve Co. (eye salve), 1928. 7. M. E. Potter & Co. (eczema ointment), 1922. 8. Bio-Labro Co. (cough medicine), 1928. 9. Mellière Labs (anemia medicine), 1928.

1. International Hi Gypsy Co. (salve), 1922. 2. Opazel Labs (medicated cream), 1922.
3. Pennsylvania Glass Co. (medicine droppers), 1928. 4. Jackson Medicine Co. (digestive
powder), 1922. 5. Dorothy Gray (chin straps), 1928. 6. Union Pharmacol Co. (general tonics),
1920. 7. Margueritte A. Wanderly (salve for feet), 1922. 8. Guinea Products Co. (ointment),
1922. 9. Standard Products Co. (liniment), 1928.

DURO

1

CLOROX

2

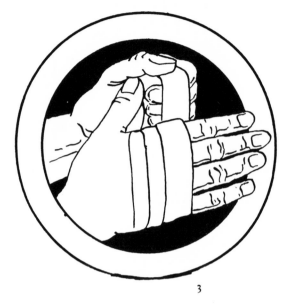

3

Flapper

4

5

LeRoy

6

WOODEN SHOE

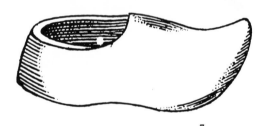

7

Venerex
TRADE MARK
PROPHYLACTIC

8

SPINOLA

9

1. Allstead Pharmacy Co. (antiseptic for gums), 1928. **2.** Clorox Chemical Co. (bleaching antiseptic), 1928. **3.** C. A. Mosso Labs (antiseptic liniment), 1926. **4.** Laddie A. Williston (astringent), 1922. **5.** Artificial Ear Drum Co. (ear drums), 1924. **6.** LeRoy Medicine Co. (laxative tablets), 1923. **7.** Sterns-Eddy Co. (Haarlem oil capsules), 1922. **8.** Jack F. Katz (prophylactic and preventative), 1928. **9.** Sebastian Spinner (tonic for stomach), 1924.

1. Krany Mfg. Co. (liniment), 1926. 2. Hennafoam Corp. (cough syrup), 1922. 3. Panagiota Kekas (eyedrops), 1925. 4. Stanco, Inc. (nose and throat spray), 1928. 5. Pre-Ven-Tion Labs (prophylactic ointment), 1927. 6. Mibalm Co. (medicine), 1927. 7. Sherwood Petroleum Co. (mineral oil), 1928. 8. Henry G. Seyfarth (laxative, cough and cold remedy), 1922.